MY VIEW FROM THE PORCH

By Bob O'Rear

Introduction

My wife, Kathy and I retired and moved to the North Georgia Mountains five years ago. This year I turned 75 years of age, and I guess that's supposed to be some kind of milestone. I've never been 75 before, and I'm not sure how you are supposed to feel and act. I know some time ago I quit being overly self-conscious and now I pretty much speak what's on my mind. I mean I still try to be respectful to people, but being 75 should have some benefits. I have learned a few things, like you can't call people on the channel selector, and never I mean never keep your toothpaste and Preparation H in the same drawer. I rarely lose my car in the parking lot since I've discovered how that beeping thingy works, and my wife doesn't have to page me quite as often at the grocery store. They have made the cars much easier to start now. I just have to be sure I am getting in mine.

Every morning I start my day on the front porch with my cup of coffee and my German Shepherd. Mattie. I spend my time in prayer, reflection, and sometimes just remembering. I've been unable to acquire a friend to share this time and old stories with me, so lucky you, I've decided to share some thoughts and stories with you. I am hopeful that reading this book will cause you to reflect, laugh and remember past times and pleasant memories as we share "My View From The Porch."

Mountain Mornings

Every morning I begin each day (weather permitting) on my front porch with my cup of coffee and my German Shepherd, Mattie. I have a beautiful view of the North Georgia mountains. One morning I experienced something that led me to write a poem about it. I hope you enjoy the poem.

The morning mist rises gently from the valley below, slowly revealing the distant mountain ranges. Eventually, it will yield its existence completely to the early morning sun.
The sun brings with it the rooster's wake-up call
Another morning begins in the North Georgia mountains.

The smell of fresh brewed coffee begins to stimulate the senses. As we begin to embrace the challenges of the day, our dog becomes aware of our arousing And greets us with tail eagerly waging.

The birds outside, always among the earliest risers and hardest workers Begin each day with a song.
We swing out of bed and our feet touch the wooden floor, as we make the final commitment to face the day.

Bob O'Rear

Driving Instructor

I am thinking about getting a sign for the back of our Highlander that says student driver since the person that is usually riding with me these days has become a self-appointed driving instructor.

For most of our marriage we had our own cars, and were usually not riding together, but since we retired qnd Kathy has no special ed students to teach, well. You see Kathy took drivers ed 50 years ago, and since I only took the Richard Petty course, obviously she is more qualified to share the rules of the road with me, whether solicited or not.

I really have consciously tried to slow down, and I can pretty much anticipate the things she will bring up by now. Things like slow down because you know the police are usually hiding around this stretch; but sometimes I get caught up in what we are talking about, or my own thoughts and forget. I have tried to critique her driving as well, but have learned she does not want to hear it. In fact one time after I had knee surgery and she had to do all the driving, she got so tired of my attempts to help get us to where we were going five seconds faster she came up with a plan.

She borrowed a tape recorder from a friend and put it under the front seat. The plan, of course, was to record all my comments, and let me hear how I sounded all the time. Constantly telling her how to drive. Well, I had decided that since she was going to ignore all my great advice and basically everything I said, which was very frustrating to me, that I just wasn't going to say anything. Score one for the home team.

I don't know if this is the case for all couples, but my style of driving is to drive defensively. I don't trust other drivers to not pull out in front of me or to not come over in my lane without warning, so I drive defensively. Another big difference is how I look down the road, observing whether I need to change lanes, slow down, etc. In other words, anticipating ahead of time.

One of the things I used to do that I suspect a lot of men do when taking a family trip, is that when we take a long trip, I have a pretty good idea, traffic permitting, the shortest amount of time it should take to make the trip, stops and all. This rarely worked out because of circumstances beyond my control like the bladders of three small boys and stops taking way longer than necessary. I know this doesn't help my case, but that was my plan.

Kathy said I need to put a section about this in the book, so here it is. I realize that someday the family will come to me and say it's time to give up my keys. The only driving I will do then is when I sit behind the wheel of our car in the garage and go rum, rum. Until then, if you are out driving and you see me coming, either get over or go on.

Television

My attraction to television goes back over 70 years. Being an only child who was responsible for his own entertainment most of the time, it was the perfect place to escape to. My first memories of television were shows like Howdy Doody with Buffalo Bob and Captain Kangaroo. Later on I remember Saturdays with Hopalong Cassidy and Tarzan. Then there were family shows like Leave It To Beaver and Father Knows Best. Being a very impressionable boy from a broken home, I made the mistake of thinking this was how most of the other families in the world lived, and that I had been shortchanged. Fortunately as I got older, I was able to appreciate how truly blessed and loved I was, and as an adult be able to repay my grandparents for all the love and sacrifices they made for me. My mother worked hard too and along with my stepfather, Ben paid for my college education, which has helped me enjoy the career and life I have been able to live. Sadly, she died when I was 19, and we never got to really know each other as adults.

Tv then went through a copycat period. When shows became popular then the networks flooded us with similar shows or direct spinoffs. For a while tv networks flooded us with westerns. Some of my favorites were Gunsmoke, Wagon Train, Have Gun Will Travel, and The Virginian. There were a ton of others and I watched them all. Every red-blooded young boy would strap on his holster and go outside to face the bad guys.

The next phase I remember were detective and police shows like Dragnet, Hawaii Five-0 and two of the best of all time Columbo and The Fugitive. After this came all the sitcoms with their canned laughter. Show like the Mary Tyler Moore Show, The Bob Newhart Show, and The Andy Giffith Show, among so many other great shows. I wanted to mention one of my favorites The Twilight Zone as well.

There were also a ton of variety shows. Over the years it seems like everyone had a variety show. Shows like The Ed Sullivan Show, The Show of Shows, The Carol Burnett Show, the Smother Brothers, and so many other great shows. I especially looked forward to Walt Disney Presents, a true variety show that offered something new and entertaining each week.

In the 60s I went from not just wanting to play sports, but to watching them on tv as well. My early memories were of players like Jim Brown and Dick Butkus and how they dominated their sport. I have enjoyed watching so many talented players over the years, but sadly big money and greed has tarnished all phases of tv sports today. I believe that all seasons are too long, and that by the time you get to the playoffs you are not getting the players best performance, assuming they are still able to play. This could be fixed by shortening all the seasons, and thus reducing the payrolls, advertising costs, overhead, and ultimately reducing the ticket costs for the fans. I'm just saying.

Someone once said that tv dumbs us down, and I

have found that to be true (yes even in my own case). There are shows on today that have real in their title that are anything but real. The news quit reporting just the facts, and tries to influence us bases on their own bias. I have found this to be especially true on the national news stations. Even the commercials are guilty of trying to be social engineers. It's sometimes easy to forget that tv was meant to be a place to escape reality.

Today I check in on the news every day, to see what's going on, then I watch old movies or tv shows. As far as sports, I like to watch a good college football game, March Madness, or the Masters. I try to watch shows like Jeopardy, Alone and Mountain Men. But I'm not glued to the tv all the time like I used to be. I like to turn off the tv and read a good book or finish a project I have been putting off, and I find those times to be much more enlightening and productive. Remember life is what happens when you make plans.

Censorship

My life as a young boy began m the town of Red Bank, Tennessee. Red Bank was just north of Chattanooga. It wasn't a big town, but it was just the perfect size for me. I spent hours riding my bike on the sidewalks from our house to town and back. The houses were almost all one story homes of working class people. My mother and I lived with my grandparents in a two bedroom home. My mother worked as a secretary for an auto repair business, my grandfather worked at the paper mill, and my grandmother took care of the home and garden. I believe the 1950's were the most wonderful time ever for a boy to grow up in (if you were white), but I'll speak of that later.

This was a time of strong church influences, Walt Disney movies, TV shows with loving families that treated each other with respect. There were standards of conduct and decency. Today many of the movies have very vulgar language and violent and explicit scenes. Somewhere along the time I was entering my teens, censorship was portrayed as the bad guy, trying to prevent us from enjoying our music and entertainment. It was the older generation trying to prevent our generation from setting our own standards, We never saw it as trying to protect us. There is nothing wrong with a new generation charting their own course, but I have learned it is wise to listen to the advice of those who love us and have been there before, and to have some experience in life and have a working knowledge of history and the Bible before proceeding too deeply.

The biggest reason we are at the place we are today, is because we have turned too far away from God and His Word (the Bible). You see God gave us The Bible as a loving Father to help guide us and encourage us in the way we should live our lives, to help us have a life that is full of true joy, and to have a sense of fulfillment By our own rebellious nature we have chartered our own course, and found ourselves in the place we are today. This has been greatly aided by dishonest and power hungry politicians, and many of the news media that steered the news we heard and saw to fit their social agenda, and what they thought our nations priorities should be. Unfortunately this was a complete 180 degrees from what God knew and told us would be best for us and our world.

We have now come to the year 2022 where something 60 years ago was unthinkable. Attempts are being made to censor the church and to edit God's Word. Why, because Jesus is the light of the world. The Bible tell us 1n John 3:19 "Light has come into the world, but men loved darkness because their deeds were evil." It is very ironic that in this new society and it's distorted set of values, that we have gone from an attempt to censor worldly and sinful standards and live in a Christian and Bible based society to a society that tries to censor those Godly principles and standards.

Well, It Says Drive-In

I don't think young men intentionally set off to get into mischief or trouble. I mean sometimes it kind of
follows them around or just sneaks up on them when they least expect it. I was a young man of 17, hanging out with my friends Wayne and Barry. I don't know why I wasn't with my regular crowd playing football. I guess they must have had other plans. Well we were sitting around on Sunday afternoon kind of bored. A true recipe for trouble.

The subject came up about the new drive-in that had just opened on Hwy 153. I shared that just a few nights ago, when I was hanging out with the regular crowd, we found a way to sneak in without paying. This time my friend Mike was driving, and everything went off without a hitch. Wayne was driving his mother's 49 Chevy, and suggested that since I was familiar with the plan, that I drive. Do you see a problem developing here? I said okay, because I was sure I could handle this with no problem. I know you see trouble written all over this, but a 17 year old doesn't think that way. He just sees this as another adventure.

The drive-in has a long common road going down it that was used for entering and leaving. The secret was that you just drove down the road like you were going to the entrance, and at the last second you killed the lights, hit the gas and drove in the exit. Then you quickly found a vacant spot, killed the engine and played innocent.

Well everything was going according to plan, except when I accelerated I started spinning out in the gravel. I touched the brakes to steady the car, and then surprise! Wayne had failed to mention the brakes didn't work very well, if at all. There I went race car fans plowing right through the sheet metal. I tried to put it in reverse and get out of there, but the engine quickly died. By then the drive-in manager had appeared.

Two other things I wanted to share. On the movie screen at the exact same time was a scene of moonshiners being chased by revenuers across a mountain road, and right then as if on cue, I come crashing through the sheet metal beside the movie screen. Everybody was cheering and saying all right. Thankfully, there was no damage to Wayne's mothers car. The best part was how nice the manager was. I was expecting to get the butt chewing I deserved, but instead he could not have been nicer. First he wanted to make sure we were okay. Then he said he would have their maintenance man fix the damages, and only charge me for the materials ($70). His kindness made a really great impression on me about how to treat people. I like to think I gave new meaning to the term drive-in.

My Georgia Mountain Home

I was born to a restless spirit
With a soul that was destined to roam. My life spent
searching for answers
To questions I did not know.
My searching has led me to a place Lost somewhere in
my dreams
Where the seasons paint classic pictures And the
birds are united in song.
I've followed my heart as it led me to My Georgia
mountain home.

I awake to a majestic sunrise Over distant mountain
ranges.
Where the mountain laurel embraces Cascading
mountain streams.
A southern breeze blows gently Through the stately
oaks and pines. I'm finally back in the bosom
Of the place I sought so long.
I've found true peace and happiness In my Georgia
mountain home.

Traditions are honored and true
With bonds that go deep from the past. Answers to
questions are thoughtfully given To questions respect-
fully asked.
A people that I can gladly embrace With a lasting
common soul.
Love of God and family Will always be their code.
This son of the south has come to rest In my Georgia
mountain home.

11

Bob O'Rear

Who's Got The Wheel

When I was a young man growing up I was skinny and very self-conscious. I was kind of a goofy kid that just went along with the crowd. The crowd consisted mainly of my two friends David and Kelley. I never really planned anything beyond the weekend, which in middle school involved spending Friday night at Kelley's and later on trying to get a date for the drive-in. Kelley and David were much more successful in that department, but I was able to get a date from time to time. Unfortunately I was kind of a one date Harvey, and I never seemed to be able to date the same girl twice. I guess they must have had a problem with maturity or lack thereof.

Every Sunday after church and dinner, we would meet at some vacant lot or on the high school football field for a game of tackle football. I loved everything about tackle football the contact, the strategy, and especially the running. This was something I had always been very good at and in time would help to build my self-confidence. We got after it pretty good, but fortunately no one was ever seriously hurt. We didn't play dirty, just with a lot of enthusiasm. Every Sunday rain or shine we were out there. We ended up having intramural games at our high school, and our team won all our games, and were champions. Even now I miss it, and when I see some kids throwing the ball around I want to get out there. I conveniently have forgotten how all my muscles hurt until Thursday when I began to feel halfway normal again, and was ready for next Sunday's game.

Another thing we did on weekends, if we had no plans, was to just hang out together. Maybe get a few beers and ride around with the gang. On this particular weekend, I had borrowed my grandfather's station wagon and was driving. I was going about 50 mph on the inside lane of a four lane road cresting a hill. I don't remember what was said by someone in the back seat, but I must have found it interesting, so I turned around to put in my two cents worth. Taking my eyes off the road. Fortunately, David, who was riding shotgun did not. He saw we were crossing the center line grabbed the wheel, and got us back in our lane. A few seconds later another car going the other way in that lane crested the hill. David reminded me of this not too long ago. I get cold chills thinking how my life could have turned out, compared to how blessed It has been. Thank you old friend for grabbing that wheel.

Mama and Papa

When I was two years old my parents got a divorce and my mother and I moved in with my grandparents. I have no idea what we would have done if they had not taken us in. My grandparents lived in a one story two bedroom home in a working class community. As a young boy with no real experience in life you don't think much beyond your own needs and circumstances. There were many times as a young man I felt like I might have been short changed, but fortunately as I sit here today, I can say that growing up no one was more loved or blessed to be with the people who raised him than me. I can say that without reservation, I wouldn't change one thing about how I was raised.

I didn't grow up poor, I grew up rich with things money could never buy. We always had lots of love, I was taught to respect my elders, and I learned about good work ethic. Our greatest riches were our family and our faith in God.

Papa, my grandfather was from Coalmont, Tennesse. One of ten children. The last child my uncle Russell weighed 16 pounds when he was born. I think that's about the time my great grandmother hung up the closed for business sign. I don't know much about my grandfathers childhood except that he grew up on a farm and there were mules plowing and a lot of hard work. I think he was the oldest so that probably meant he had to work the hardest. When he was 19 he left home and headed over the mountain to Chattanooga picking up any work he could and eventually ending up working at Container Corporation, a paper mill. I came into the picture a little over twenty years later. I used to sleep up in the attack every night. I would pull down the stairs walk over the cold linoleum floor and go to bed on my featherbed. It was very cold in the winter and very hot in the summer. Oh I forgot to mention that the fellow in the other bed beside me was my grandfather. He had given up his room to my mother. He used to leave for work before light every morning. I don't believe that the whole time I was up there I ever heard him leave. I just know that when I woke up he had left for work.

Mama said that there were some days when he left for work he was so sick he should have been in the hospital, but we needed the money to pay the bills. We used to open our Christmas presents every Christmas Eve. It was years later until I realized that we did that because Papa always worked Christmas day to get the double time pay. Because of his outgoing personality he was a greeter at our church. It was said of him that he never met a stranger. If he was standing beside someone at a store he would always strike up a conversation. His qualities as a man were qualities that were not lectured to me, but were modeled for me.

Mama was one of the kindest most loving people I have ever been blessed to know. She was born in Palmer, Tennessee. Her father my great grandfather farmed and ran a local store. Mama did not have an easy life either. By the time she was twelve she had

lost both her parents and her home had burned to the ground. She was moved from family to family, and on many occasions told they just didn't have room for her there. She would tearfully respond but I have nowhere else to go. When she was 19 she headed for Chattanooga where she boarded with some relatives and went to work in a box factory. One night she was fixed up on a blind date with my grandfather, and he promptly told her that he was going to marry her. Well he did. In 1927 they had my mother their only child, my mother. The childbirth was so difficult that Mama would be unable to have any more children. Things did not get any easier for in a little over a year the family faced the Great Depression. Even though I was a CFO for forty years, my greatest training field for managing money came from my grandmother. My grandmother was one of those extremely smart people who was so quiet and unassuming that you didn't realize how smart she was until you studied her body of work. She taught herself how to play the organ and played it at church for over 40 years. I know now she must have read a lot, I just never saw her reading much just working all the time. Cooking, tending her garden, sewing, etc. Sadly in 1966 she would face her greatest heartbreak when my mother, her only child, died of cancer. For all the years after this when I went off to college, served in the Army, or after I had moved to Atlanta, when I came home, she would always have my favorite meal ready. She was the best cook ever. She was kind and loving, and I never heard her complain or speak ill of others. In Proverbs 31:26-31is a verse befitting Mama. She
Speaks with wisdom, and faithful instruction is on

her tongue. She watches over the affairs of her household and does not eat the bread of idleness. Her children arise and call her blessed; her husband also and he praises her. Many women do noble things, but you surpass them all. Charm is deceptive and beauty is fleeting, but a woman who fears the Lord is to be praised. Give her the reward she has earned".

I was very, blessed to take care of my grandparents with the help of some great neighbors as they lived into their 90s. I believe that you can see some of both of them in me. If nothing else I think I was smart enough to finally appreciate two great role models when I saw them. Today, I am blessed and honored beyond words to be their grandson.

Kathy and The Boys

1979 was to prove to be a very significant year in my life. I was entrenched in a job as CFO for a restaurant franchise that would sustain me and my family for 40 years and I had just purchased my first house. There was one problem, however, not only did I not have a family to share it with, I didn't even have a girl friend much less a wife. I was 32 years old and convinced that all the best flowers had already been picked, and I may have to face the possibility that the family I had always dreamed of was not to be.

Enter stage left some friends that fixed me up on a blind date with Kathy. It wasn't love at first sight, but we sure did like what we saw. I think from that point on neither one of us wanted to be with anyone else. I got to know Kathy as a very sweet loving person that was even more beautiful inside than she was outside. The key for me and any future marriage was always that even though I wasn't living the Christian life style very much at the time, 1frew that if I did get married we would raise our family in a Christian home. We were both completely on the same page as far as that was concerned. We began attending a local church and joined a Sunday school class with several couples our age. It was on the
way home from church that I made my first and on-

ly proposal of marriage. It was not as romantic as wished it would be. I knew I was capable of something better, but fortunately she accepted and we were married on January 12, 1980.

Kathy has proven to be a better wife and person than I could have ever hoped for or deserved. We were blessed to be able to have her stay at home with the boys until they were all ready for school. She then was able to work in the school systems as a teacher's aide, which worked out well during the summers. She has a very loving and generous heart, and quickly found her place in working with special needs kids. This a very challenging job both physically and mentally. There is no one size fits all in getting through to these kids. Each one is unique, and I have been so impressed with how Kathy has been able to get through to all her kids with creative ways using computers and other means. She loved them all and never gave up on any of them, and they knew it.

I'm convinced that we all have a soul, and when you've been married to someone for almost 43 years you have a clear understanding of what that person's soul is like. I am truly blessed to see the beautiful person that lives within the soul of my wife, Kathy. We have now begun the next chapter of our life together, as we have both retired and moved to our mountain home with our two dogs in north Georgia. We have now been here for almost five years, and it has proven to be even better than we could have ever hoped for. Love to Kathy.

We have been blessed to be the parents of three

sons, that God has entrusted to our care for 30-40 years. As you know there are a lot of books out there about how to raise your children, but we have found the Bible to be the greatest resource about how to raise your children. That being said, I don't know why you'd be asking me anyway, since Kathy did most of the heavy lifting. I mostly provided financial and emotional stability. I not saying that I didn't pitch in, it's just only fair to say Kathy did most of the work.

Our oldest son was Casey. He was born September 6, 1981. He was a good looking tow haired boy, active and healthy, except for one thing. He had some allergy asthma problems when he was young that took a while to get properly diagnosed. We spent quite a few nights in emergency rooms until we got a handle on it. As with most firstborns, Casey and his mother have always been close, and still remain close today. We are now blessed to share our love with Casey's wife, Eve, and our three sweet grandchildren, Reese, Alex and Scottie. Today we are extremely proud of the man he's grown to be. He's a beloved son, husband and father. He's a person that is liked and appreciated by a good circle of friends, and he's a valued and respected employee at the company he works for. And he's also a decorated veteran of the war in Afghanistan. We love you son, and are proud of you.

Our next two sons, John T. and Brad are twins, born on December 28, 1985. They were six weeks premature. So that when they came home they were on heart monitors, and had to be given medicine every three hours. Needless to say these were challenging times for young parents. It's kind of a blur now, but this is when Kathy really earned her stripes. Growing up we tried to encourage them to participate in different things, but they preferred to be home boys.

After high school you can imagine our surprise when John T. informed us that he wanted to enlist in the Marines. This home boy that we couldn't get to try anything wanted to be a Marine. Well Lance Corporal John T. O'Rear went on to earn a Meritorious Mast for driving a Humvee 17,000 miles without an incident in Iraq. He has since expanded our circle of love and family with the addition of his wife, Kristin and our sweet grandchildren Aidan and Abbie. He is also a valued and trusted employee at his place of work, and an admired and beloved person to his circle of friends, We are very proud of the man he has become. We love you son.

Our last son was kind of a late bloomer, but has made a great deal of progress in the last few years, Brad had to have three surgeries for scar tissue that had adhered to his intestines from surgery he had when he was an infant. It seemed that every time he was making progress he would be derailed by another surgery. The last time was when he was in basic training in the Air Force. He was given a medical discharge and had to come home facing another surgery. Fortunately the last surgery seems to have gotten the job done, and the last few years have been very positive for Brad. He has found a good job as a lab technician and is a very valued employee. He married late in life, like I did, but found a jewel in Amanda. This past year they were blessed with a beautiful baby girl, Madison. We love you son, and are very proud of the man you've become.

On the Porch
With Jeff

I am very excited today, because Mattie and I are sharing our front porch and a cup of coffee with my old friend, Jeff Foxworthy. We love to sit around and talk about life, our faith, and bounce around any creative comedy ideas that come to mind. It's never dull and you never know where our crazy minds are going to take us. Okay, I really don't know Jeff. Actually, I've never even met him. I did see him perform one time, though. I thought that since this was my view from the porch, I could pretend Jeff was here.

I've seen him on tv on many occasions, and by all accounts he seems to be a very grounded down to earth fellow, with a strong faith and an incredible and very creative sense of humor. I mean when it get's down to it, we are really like two peas in a pod. I mean I do have a strong faith, and I like to think I have a very creative sense of humor. Whether I do have this creative sense of humor, I'll let you be the judge.

From time to time I come up with an idea that I think would be a good tv venue for Jeff and his talents, and hey since he's already been in fourteen Jeff Foxworthy tv shows, what difference is one more going to make. The idea I came up with today, is a spinoff of the tv show Alone. Alone is an inter-

23

esting show where a group of approximately ten participants that are skilled natural survivors (at least that's what the disclaimer says), compete against each other. They are all taken to a remote location full of bears and other predators, where the temperatures plummet to freezing conditions. They then attempt to show who can catch the least fish and wild game, eventually having to live on a diet of water and strange looking stuff they dig out of the ground.

They all build shelters, some of which are very creative, and then proceed to see who can last the longest. They are almost always on camera, so they must think they have to be entertaining.

Sometime they sing songs they have written, which is great if you like songs that make no sense, and are being sung by someone that can't carry a tune in a bucket. Towards the end of the show when the participants have thinned out (literally), you get to share in the human suffering of people that have lost half their body weight and all of their mind. One recent participant thought he was Millard Fillmore, and had signed ten executive orders before they could get him out of there.

Well enter Jeff and his new spinoff show that we will call Abandoned. This show has a slightly different concept. You are not given a tap out button to come and rescue you when you are ready to give up, in other words you are truly on your own kid. Another change is that the prize money will not be $500,00. Quite frankly, it will have to be a little bit less. We'll have to see if the show is going to take off or not. I guess it will just have to be a surprise at the end of the show for the winner to see just how much we've been able to put together.

Okay, here are a few other ideas for after we inject Jeff into the show; along with some of his creative comedy genius. The first scene will be of Jeff inside his leanto he has built, and is very proud of the job he has done. The leanto itself is one of the most pathetic looking pieces of construction you have ever seen. It looks like something put together by a drunk chimpanzee in a wind storm. Jeff, however, is inside bragging about it, when the whole thing collapses on him.

This is the time to get the old gang together to compete against each other. Cletus Bridgewater, Big Thelma Hightower, Richard Running Wolf, one of the Robbison twins,and Big Earl. Get the whole gang back together again. As you can see, my idea needs a lot of work, and that's why I'm not working on my fifteenth show for myself. But I figure with Jeffs creative talent we could have a hit on our hands. Okay, I know it's totally unrealistic, but a morning on the porch with Jeff, now that would be incredible.

Bob O'Rear

Volunteers

I wanted to write a section on volunteering since it is an area that has been so personally rewarding and fulfilling in my life. It is also an area of great need in our community and world that many times goes unnoticed by us. An example of this where there is a need we may be totally unaware of for example is something we did in our previous church several years ago. Some of the members wanted to start a program where we prepared summer lunches for some of the children in our community. Well this seemed like a nice gesture to me, but certainly was never an issue in my life growing up, but the people organizing the project told us that many of the kids in our community came to school in the fall weighing less than they did when they left school for the summer. This meant that without their school lunches, they were not getting enough to eat and the proper nutrition they needed in the summer. This was something that was occurring right here in our community that I was totally oblivious to. No child should ever go to bed hungry, period. Certainly not in our own community.

I have volunteered in a lot of different areas over the years, and one of the great blessings I have experienced is the privilege of working along side some of the most caring and dedicated people you would ever want to know. For ten years I volunteered at the North Gwinnett Co-op. They offered food to the needy families in our community, as well as a thrift store where donations of mostly clothes were offered at a very good price. Our church began the co-op, and I was really drawn to it by how effective it was at finding so many creative ways of acquiring the food and clothes, and getting them to the people of need in our community. Here again I was unaware of what a great need there was.

My first area of volunteering was as a member of the Executive Park Kiwanis Club, and then as a Scoutmaster for several years. There are a lot of great experiences and memories I have along with friendships that were formed that I still treasure. Being a Scoutmaster of a new troop was very challenging, but the commitment and enthusiasm of the boys made it all worthwhile.

Most of the other areas I volunteered in were at my church Sugar Hill UMC. This included going on missions trips, being a youth leader, singing with a men's group and in the choir, and serving on many committees many times as chairman. The committee thing was not always my first choice, but in the end it was a very necessary part of getting the job done. I also worked with a group that volunteered to do home repairs for people of our community, that needed help.

Another program I volunteered with was in the Emmaus community for six years. This was one of the most rewarding experiences of my spiritual life and growth.

Every day we will see opportunities where people really need our help. Here is where we hear those two voices. One voice gives us a long list of excuses not to get involved, but the better voice encourages us to pitch in and see where we can help. Some people spend their whole life sitting on the sidelines complaining offering excuses; never willing to offer their time, talents, and compassion to say can I help. This is not about you being taken advantage of. It is about you giving something back for all that free air you have been breathing for all these years. I encourage you to listen to the song "A Few Good Men" by the Gaithers, and listen to your heart.

Old Friends

I was sitting here on the porch thinking about old times and old friends. My earliest memory of good friends was of David and Kelly in middle school and high school. That was before we went our separate ways and didn't hang out together almost every weekend. Kelly's folks had a small shed behind there house with an attic and a small mattress in it. This is where we started most every Friday night. We would roam the streets of Red Bank, not getting into any real mischief, just hanging out. One of the things we did was to sit on the top of the furniture store watching the occasional car go by, and just talk about stuff. Whenever we started getting interested in girls, that was a primary subject. Then later on when we were driving, it would be trips to the drive in. They introduced me to some of the current music and gave me the facts of life talk. That really got my attention. It was about this time that we started playing tackle football every Sunday afternoon on some vacant lot or on our school's football field. I'm sure we got into a little mischief back then too, but boys don't think of it that way or look that far ahead, we just look at it as another adventure. They both made the two hour drive to see me graduate from college, something I still appreciate and treasure. David and I were both best men at our weddings. Thanks for the great memories old friends.

Well in 1965 after graduating from Red Bank High School, I went off to attend college at Tennessee

Tech University to become an engineer. I lived in a house off campus because all the dorms were full. College is usually the first time away from home for many of us, and if you forget what your priorities are you will be home in short order. It took me a while to learn how to study, but I eventually figured it out. I also discovered the game of pool, my freshman year; and had to go to summer school to keep from flunking out. I made really good grades in summer school, changed my major to accounting, and really grew up a lot. The next three years I continued to grow and mature. My friends in college were Jimmy, Bill and Harry, a friend from high school that would later become my roommate in Atlanta. Jimmy would graduate as a chemical engineer, Bill would become a CPA, and Harry an Industrial Engineer. These guys provided me with a good stable friendship, and a lot of good times and memories. Bill was a bit of a character, and that's a lot for me to say, all things considered. Jimmy was a fun guy too and one of the nicest people I have ever known. I was really luck to have these guys as roommates and friends during
my college years.

After I graduated from college, I was drafted into thearmy and served most of my time at Ft. Bragg in the 82nd Airborne. My best two friends and roommates then were Bob and Dan.

They were also college graduates and great guys whose friendship helped the next two years go well. All three of us made it to the rank of sergeant in two years, which is very rare. I had a Chevy II with a 327 in it, way too much car for me. You can bet they have some stories of me behind the wheel. I had lost touch with both of them, but was able to find Bob last month, and had a great time talking to him, sharing old memories and filling in the years. Hope to be able to see him and his wife Vickie soon.

I lived the single life in Atlanta the next eight years, and shared some great times and memories with new and old friends. After I got married my circle of friends and priorities changed dramatically. We had joined a Sunday school class with couples our own age, and everyone seemed to be having babies at the same time. They were a great influence in helping shape me into the person I am today. In 1986 we moved to another house and found a new church at Sugar Hill Methodist Church. The men and women of this church would have a profound effect upon my life for the next thirty years. As I attempt to name a few, I apologize in advance for those I may omit. People that have meant so much to me in my spiritual growth. I remember Jim and Jan, Toby and Paula, Bob and Barb, Steve, Bill, Joe. Miles and Evelyn, Geraldine, Mark, Jeff and Sarah, Nathan, Leo, Corban, and so many other men and women at the church that have meant so much to me. These are just a few of the men and women that inspired me by their wo.rds and actions to be a better Christian man.

As I sit here today on my front porch, I would be greatly remiss, if I did not mention some of the new friends we've made since we moved here. Friends like Billy, the best POA president any subdivision could ever ask for, and a man that can mix with just about anyone. We are also blessed by the new group of friends we have made at our new church home. All of these folks have grown up together here, but they sure made Kathy and I feel like a part of the family. I know five years of living in this community can't put us on equal footing with people they have known for 70 years, but they sure have made us feel welcome. Thanks again for helping us feel at home, and a special thanks to my old friend, Walter who we lost this year.

Without old friends to share our life with, life would seem awfully empty. Mark Twain once said "Carrying a cat by the tail will teach you something you can learn in no other way". Which has absolutely nothing to do with the rest of this section on friends. I wanted to get it in, and couldn't find anyplace else to put it. Hey, why am I apologizing? This is my book after all. Thank you Lord for good friends, one of lives greatest blessings.

Blessed Assurance

The Bible is full of so many verses where God promises us that He will always love us, provide for us, and never leave or forsake us. I thought I would share a few of my favorites.

"Be strong, and of a good courage, fear not, nor be afraid of them; for the Lord thy God, He it is that doth go with thee; He will not fail thee, nor forsake thee."
Duet. 31:6

"Fear thou not; for I am with thee: be not dismayed; for I am thy God. I will strengthen thee; yea, I will help thee, yea I will uphold thee with the right hand of My righteousness.
Isaiah 41:10

"For I am persuaded, that neither death, nor life, nor angels, nor principalities, nor powers, nor things present, nor things to come, nor heights, nor depths, nor any other creature can separate us from the love of God, which is in Christ Jesus, our Lord."
Romans 8:38-39

""Be careful for nothing, but in everything by prayer and supplication with thanksgiving let your requests be made known unto God. And the peace of

God which passeth all understand, shall keep your hearts and minds through Christ Jesus."
Phil 4:6-7

"The Lord is my shepherd I shall not want. He maketh me to lie down in green pastures; He leadeth me beside still waters. He restores my soul..."
Psalm 23:1-3

"Which hope we have, like an anchor or the soul; both sure and steadfast..."
Hebrews 6:19

"Trust in the Lord with all thine heart; and lean not unto thine own understanding. In all thy ways acknowledge Him, and he shall direct thy paths."
Proverbs 3:5-6

"But they that wait upon the Lord shall renew their strength; they shall mount up with wings as eagles; they shall run, and not be weary; they shall walk, and not faint."
Isaiah 40:31

"I can do all things through Christ, who strengtheneth me."
Phil 4:13

Abortion

This has been a very emotional subject for many years, and most people have sat back with different opinions. Some have chosen to straddle the fence, but since the recent ruling by the Supreme Court in which they overturned Roe vs Wade I believe everyone will now have to make a stand. I'm sure most women could care less about the opinion of some 75 year old man on his porch in the mountains is, but like I say I think we are at the point in history where we must make a stand, one way or the other.

I realize for those who have gone through the process of having an abortion, or for the case of an old friend who as a young doctor performed some, this is an very delicate and personal subject than can be extremely painful to discuss. Please believe that my intention is never to cause you further hurt, or stir up painful memories. I realize, also that there are many different circumstances that have and will cause young women to consider an abortion from young teenage girls to women who just aren't ready to have a child at this time, or because of bad judgement do not want to marry and have a child by it's father.

I can truthfully say that I have no interest whatsoever in telling any women what they should do with their body. The main difference seems to be that those who believe in pro choice are so angry because they think that is what us pro life advocates are saying, but we are not. We are speaking out for that other life that is living inside pregnant women who are considering an abortion, The precious little baby that has no voice in this decision, the little child that is given no choice.

You will find no place in scripture where Jesus or the Bible advocates taking the life of this baby as acceptable. This country has been in a moral war for many years, and abortion has been the point of the spear. I couldn't feel stronger about any subject than I do about this. I wanted this book to be mostly full of humor and encouraging things, but in light of where we are as a country, and how important I think this issue is to our future, I just didn't see how I could leave it out.

I will close with a final observation. I was watching tv last year when a press conference was being held at the Virginia state capitol. They were standing there laughing, and high fiving the passage of a bill that allowed full term abortions. I mean seconds before that baby was to come out of the womb it was now legal to kill it, and they thought that was a wonderful thing. I was sitting there with tears in my eyes thinking about that precious baby who would never have a chance to be whatever they could be.

Elections

We have a big election coming up in a few months, critical to the future of our nation. I know we hear this at every election, but I think all elections are important, and I would like to give you some ideas and principles to consider in choosing your candidate before you vote. If you don't want to put any thought about who you will vote for and why, I suggest you give your brain a rest and just not vote at all. It is not my attempt here to suggest who you should vote for or what party you should support. I am trying to give you some suggestions and ideas to consider regarding all the candidates before you vote.

The first thing I would suggest is that you never, never, never vote for a candidate solely based on their tv commercials. These commercials are almost always filled with half-truths, and in many cases out right lies. I also don't like the debate format. The candidates are not asked the same questions, and their opponents keep interrupting them or give them the hard stare. The closest one to being fare I have seen was on the old Mike Huckabee show, where three questioners asked each individual candidate the exact same questions and gave the candidate several minutes at the end to say why they believe they would be the voters best choice, while the other candidates were back stage. Another thing to watch for which is particularly annoying to me, is when the candidates are asked a question they will start off by saying I'm glad you asked me that question or good question and then proceed to ramble on using their campaign talking points, and never answer the question. They want to be the leaders of one of the most powerful nations on earth, will not speak up and tell you where they stand on a key issue.

I believe the campaigns have become more like an episode of American Idol instead of what it should be, a job interview. We should be voting on resume not personality, After one of the recent presidents left office the New York Times, that had conveniently ignored these facts while he was in office, stated that when you looked at his lifes body of work and lack of any meaningful accomplishments, he really was not qualified for the job. But boy was he a smooth talker. Another thing to consider is if a candidate is an incumbent and he or she spends all their time attacking their opponent, instead of talking about all the things they have accomplished while in office is a red flag to me.

I also think there is way too much money being spent on campaigns now, and I am troubled by how much of it is coming from places and people outside our state. It is also troubling that while watching so many interviews of people on the street, their·reasons for voting for their candidate, and their apparent lack of knowledge of history is very troubling. I believe you should have to pass a fifth grade civics test to vote. Look at so many of the protesters that want to completely tear down this nation and the principles
it stands for and rebuild it into something they don't understand at all, and makes no sense like

Socialist Democracy. These people are not builders, they just like to tear down things like statues.

I really wish people would become true students of history. I wish they would take time to read good, accurate history books and historical biographies about the men and women that founded this nation the sacrifices they made to build this country, and the principles on which it was founded. I pledge allegiance to the flag of the United States of America, and to the republic for which it stands. One nation under God, indivisible, with liberty and justice for all.

Bob O'Rear

So Proudly We Hail

The flag hangs quietly from it's post In the early morning sun.
Evenually the morning breeze Will cause it to gently flutter.

We will observe how proud And majestic it looks before us. A symbol of freedom
Unlike any other.

It will remind us of the Ultimate sacrifice made by So many here and in faraway places The oh so costly price of freedom.

Perhaps as some young warrior Was breathing his last breath, And so deeply longing for home, He looked up and his last view Was of this flag.

As he went to his final sleep And embraced the hand of God.

Trips to Wyoming

When my son, Casey graduated from high school in 2000, I decided a father son trip would be a cool idea. I had always wanted to go out west to Yellowstone Park, and I thought sharing this with my son would be a great experience. So we flew out to Salt Lake City rented a convertible, and started our adventure. My plan was to drive up through Utah and Idaho to the western entrance of Yellowstone Park and spend two nights here. The first day we toured the northern end of Yellowstone all the way up into Montana and back. The openness and beauty was just breathtaking. Not even the slightest sense of being closed in. We saw beautiful mountains nd waterfalls, and wild animals like bison, moose, grizzly bears, eagles, and many more.

The first two days were just incredible, and was only going to get better. The next day we toured the southern part of Yellowstone, and saw old not so faithful. I guess he just didn't want to show the old geyser off that day. We left Yellowstone and entered the Grand Teton National Park. The view of Lake Teton with the snow capped Grand Teton Mountains behind it is still one of the most beautiful sights I have ever seen, and one of my most treasured memories.

We then proceeded to Jackson Hole, Wyoming for

our next adventure. The next evening we boarded a raft to spend an overnight adventure going down the Snake River. The evening ride was very calm and peaceful as we were able to enjoy the beautiful scenery as we paddle to our campsite. The young man who cooked for us was trained as a professional chef, and the food was excellent. In the morning, after breakfast, we headed out for the more adventurous part of the trip. This was the part where we went through the rapids. These were relatively mild compared to the Ocoee River, which I have been on five times, but the experience, none the less, was very memorial.

The next day we left Jackson Hole and drove through parts of Wyoming and Utah on our way back to Salt Lake City and the plane ride home. This drive was very beautiful in it's own right, and helped to cap off a great week. We took turns driving all week, and from Casey's comments, I know he was able to appreciate all the natural beauty and adventure I had hoped he would experience. It sure was everything and more I hoped it would be.

Five yea;s later when the twins graduated I took them on the same trip. Covering the same route, and visiting most of the same stops. There are certain times of the year when it rains a lot and the traffic is heavier, so my decision to go in early June before the classes let out farther west proved to be a good one. I hope John and Brad enjoyed the trip. I believe they did.

Nothing can compare to seeing and experiencing this the first time, but to this day the trip Kathy and I shared out there was our favorite vacation. We rented a new red Chevrolet Camaro convertible and covered much the same route that I had in our previous trips, but sharing it with Kathy made it special. In stead of rafting we spent a day on horse-back. Sitting up on a mountain eating lunch looking at the Grand Tetons is still one of our favorite memories.

Music

I wanted, I guess needed is a better word to put a section about music in the book, because it has been such an important part of my life. My love of music goes back over 60 years. I took piano lessons until I was thirteen, and played in the school band for six years. I sang In church choirs for many years and with a men's group called Men of Praise. I was blessed to grow up in the greatest period of music ever, the 60s and 70s. I was also blessed to have lived long enough to have discovered a wide variety of great music that I hadn't recognized or appreciated when I was younger.

My first love for music began when I heard a rhythm and blues song by Otis Redding called "I've Been Loving you Too Long." Since that time, through the years, I have been able to appreciate the talent and beauty of so many different types of music and so many very talented artists. When you like the sound and words to a song and it really speaks to you inside, then you are really on too something. One of my favorite possessions is my ipod. I was able a few years ago to put hundreds of my favorite songs from a variety of different styles of music on it.

I really enjoy it when Kathy and I go on an extended drive playing it. As I said, it has a wide variety of songs, rhythm and blues, gospel music, country music, jazz, easy listening, classical, love songs, and a lot of golden oldies. Some of my favorite artists are in R&B Otis Redding, Aretha Franklin Ray Charles, Sam Cooke, Al Green, Jerry Butler, James lngram,and Booker T. and the MGs. In country I love Merle Haggard, Patsy Cline, Alabama, Johnny Cash, Willie Nelson, the Statler Brothers, Books and Dunn, Hank Williams, George Jones, Vince Gill, Alan Jackson, Emmylou Harris, and Dolly Parton. Easy listening would include Frank Sinatra, Ella Fitzgerald, Bobby Hackett, Nat King Cole, Perry Como, and Jacky Gleason.

When it gets to the oldies, there are so many songs and artists I like, I'll just name a few to get some idea of my favorites. The Righteous Brothers, the Temptations, the Beach Boys, the Eagles, Steeley Dan, Bread, Johnny Rivers, Carol King, Don Mclean and so many other talented singers and groups there is not room to list them. I just had to put this section in the book to share my great love for music and so many talented artists that have entertained m·e in such a special way over the years. I know many of you reading this know what I'm talking about, since you have experienced the same thing.

Even today I am discovering new artists and songs that I somehow missed in years past. Artist and songs like "Mister Dieingly Sad" by the Critters with it's beautiful harmony, the soulful "Every Little Bit Hurts" by Brenda Holloway, that she recorded as a teenager, and "Farther Along." An old gospel song with a powerful message. I can always count on my good friend, Dale, whose knowledge and love of music surpasses mine to share a new song from time to time I had never heard before.

There are so many songs and artist I did not mention that have really touched me over the years, and still do. I know that many of you reading this have had the same experience, and understand why I had to include this section.

Where Are All the Christians?

This is a letter to the editor that I wrote in response to this question that was in a previous editorial. I recognized that it was simply an attempt to bait me, but I wrote it for those open minded people that needed to hear an answer.

I would like to reply to a recent letter titled· "Where Are the Christians?" Most of the good ones I know are humble, caring people who never seek the spotlight. They volunteer their time and resources at the food banks and thrift stores, helping mentor and teach young people, going on local and world mission trips to help people in need. You probably didn't notice them, because they are not trying to draw any attention to themselves. They are just trying to serve, lift up and love others as the Bible teaches.

Of course, you can't be a very good Christian if you don't try to study and follow what the Bible teaches. As it says in 2 Timothy 3:16, "All scripture is God-breathed and is useful for teaching, rebuking, correcting and training in righteousness, so that a man of God may be thoroughly equipped for every good work." A lot of people today want to pick and choose the parts of the Bible they are comfortable with and want to follow, but we must trust that the way God teaches us in His Word is the best way to have true joy and to be good ambassadors for Christ.

I would encourage everyone to go to the Bible daily to learn about God's plan and love for each of us. You my want to start with the Gospel of John, and learn about Jesus and who He really is. Learn about a God who loves us so much that He would send His own Son, Jesus to die for us. A Jesus that wants to nurture that relationship with us on a daily walk. Let us grow in this relationship as followers of Jesus Christ, so that we can share that love. As it says in Matthew 5:16"...let your light shine before men, that they may see your good deeds and praise your Father in Heaven."

Sense of Humor

I cannot possibly imagine living my life of 75 years without my faith in God and my sense of humor. I know there are people who sadly seem to not possess any signs of faith or sense of humor. They seem to take themselves and life way too seriously. Content to live a life that is by all appearances to be totally devoid of joy or laughter. I'm not trying to ignore the pain and suffering that some people have been or are currently going through. I simply saying that a life totally devoid of faith and laughter is not a physically or mentally healthy thing. I remember one time when I was going through a rough stretch and somebody said something over the radio that appealed to my wacky sense of humor, and I laughed out loud. It then occurred to me that it had been well over a month since I had laughed at anything or even smiled for that matter. So I thought I would share some of the many people and things that have appealed to my sense of humor over the years. Hopefully they will trigger some memories that have touched your funnybone over the years.

I'll start out with some of the comedians and movies that I have loved. Starting back way before I was even born there were the movies of Buster Keaton, Laurel and Hardy, and W. C. Fields among others. All of their work was comic genius, but memories of Oliver Hardy's yell when he suffered one of his many falls, and W.C. fields in The Bank Dick still crack me up.

Later on, there were so many movies with great comedians like it's a Mad, Mad, Mad, Mad World, The Russians Are Coming, The Flim-Flam Man, Young Frankenstein, Family Vacation, Animal House, Caddyshack, Airplane, Silverstreak, and Without a Clue, just to name a few. Enjoying the talent of Jonathan Winters, Sid Ceaser, John Belushi are just a few of the many talented comedians I have enjoyed, but I don't want to leave out John Candy. If there was ever anything that he was in that didn't make me laugh or lift my spirits, I can't remember what it was.

Of course tv provided us with so many talented comedians some of whom I have already mentioned. Who can forget the Carol Burnett Show with Carol, Harvey and Tim breaking us up every week. Red Skelton, Barney Fife, Flip Wilson, Johnny Carson, The Saturday Night Live cast, Robin Williams. All of the great comedians have graced us with their presence on tv at some point. And If I have left out some of your favorites it wasn't intended. All that really matters is that at some point in time they made you laugh, and that's what's important.

Another area that I have enjoyed is the comics and cartoons. We all have our favorite cartoons, but I can't imagine anyone that would not have Gary Larsen and The Far Side on their list. How he could come up with so many great cartoons for so many years is beyond my comprehension. But I sure did enjoy them and always looked forward to the next days contribution. I know you have dozens of favorites, and so do I. I'll just share one that came to mind while I was writing this. Picture a man bird hunting with two dogs. There is a dead duck floating in a small pond. Around the pond are alligators, snakes, and snapping turtles. One dog looks at the other and says you're up Red. The look on the dogs face was priceless.

For me my favorite cartoon is in a place by itself. My favorite by a mile is Wiley Coyote and the Road Runner. With all due credit to Wiley (who by all accounts was woefully misnamed), he did almost singlehandedly keep the Acme company in business. You know if you think about it, he had a really good case against Acme for defective merchandise.

Where are all those tv lawyers when you need one?

There is another area that brought a ton of entertainment to me when I was younger that I wanted to mention. When I was in my twenties living in Atlanta, we didn't have any cell phones, internet of cd players to entertain us, but we did have tv and the radio. We had two disk jockeys, Gary Mckee and Skinny Bobby Harper that were very popular. They would play all the current musical hits of the day and inject some humor and small talk. They were very good and you always enjoyed listening to them and their shows as you were driving around or to work and back. After them, a few years later, came Randy and Spiff. They were mostly a humorous talk show, that in addition to their humorous bits, had a caller that call d in with the voices of several different characters that always cracked me up.

During the 80's our professional sports teams, the Braves and Hawks were really bad, but we had a sports announcer, Skip Carey who's dry sense of humor was so funny that I would actually tune in to a Hawks game to hear him. He didn't try to paint any fake rosy picture, but called it like it was. People like myself would actually tune into the games to hear Skips humorous quips and comments. I was so thankful that in 91, he finally got to see his team, the Braves in the world series.

There was another man on the scene who called himself Ludlow Porch. He had a radio show for many years that was very entertaining. He called his followers the fun seekers, and had a whole group of regular callers like Ray- de-ator, Pretty Perky Patty, Mr. Haney and a ton of others. I called in a few times and called myself Slim Chance, but never became one of the regulars. It was a very funny and light hearted show that would always put a smile on your face.

Well they are all gone now, and I don't guess we'll ever see their like again. But at least we have our memories and their great humor they shared with us. Hopefully, I have wet your appetite to watch a funny movie, or maybe laugh out loud at some past memory. I have heard that it is good for your health, too.

My Kind of People

When Kathy and I moved to the north Georgia mountains five years ago, we already had fallen in love with its beauty and have not been disappointed. Everywhere we drive there are new landscapes to discover and embrace. After we moved here we found a small country family church that we have joined, and this has been one of our greatest discoveries. This is a church that has been here through several family generations, but from day one they made us feel so welcome, and just like family. I didn't hurt that I'd been raised by people just like this, and felt like my life had come full circle when I had settled here. Kathy, as well, has fit right in and made several new friends.

Most of the men are around my age and still have their cattle farms and businesses that keep them busy. They are very self-sufficient in their ability to build things, repair things that break down, and manage their farms and businesses. They remind me so much of some of my family members I grew up admiring as a young man. One of the greatest assets of the men and women up here that I have seen and admired is their common sense. This is a trait that seems to be in short supply in some places in today's world, but it is very abundant up here.

Some of our members were educated in universities, and all of them were educated in life. They have such a clear vision of our world and the values that are important. The pace of life is steady, but not as rushed as it was back were we moved from, which is exactly what Kathy and I were looking for. We've really enjoyed get togethers like camp meeting and our churches fifth Sunday dinners where we get together at the church fellowship hall to break bread and share some delicious home cooked food.

We have found these people to be down to earth, warm hearted people. Always ready to help a neighbor in need. In other words, my kind of people.

One of the biggest reasons I wanted to write this section of the book, was to talk about what great storytellers some of my new friends are. There is a tradition among people descended from the Appalachian mountains to pass down stories in such a way that was not only entertaining, but in a way you could really clearly visualize what they were describing. Some of the men in our church have this unique talent for storytelling, and I have enjoyed listening to their accounts of the past. These men and women and their ancestors played a key role in building this community into what it is today. They all contributed into building the roads, schools, and community we live in today.

Many of the stories are of those that have gone on before us, but they are also full of humor as well about days gone by. These were times that required hard work and perseverance, but they were also times shared around the dinner table are especially out in the woods hunting and fishing. I've been so blessed to hear stories from people like, Dickie, Ronnie and Mitchell, and my favorite, Walter who left us this year. "Precious memories, how they linger, how they ever flood my soul."

Bob O'Rear

Grace and Truth

In the Gospel of John, the story is told of Jesus teaching at the temple courts, when the Pharisees brought before Him a woman caught in adultery. They said the law of Moses commanded us to stone her, but Jesus simply bent down and began writing on the ground with His finger, while they continued to question Him. Finally, Jesus straightened up and said "if any of you is without sin, let him cast the first stone." Then Jesus bent down again and continued to write in the dirt. Finally, Jesus stood up and saw the woman standing there alone. He asked her where are your accusers, and she said they were all gone. Jesus then said "neither do I accuse you."

This is Jesus our role model sharing the grace we should all share as Christians, not condemning others. There are many who would tell us that as Christians we should never question other people's lifestyles or actions, just model ourselves after Jesus with a life of sharing grace with others. They want the story to end there. Of course, those were not Jesus final words to the woman, nor sharing grace the full extent of His ministry. His final words to her were "go and leave your life of sin." In fact, Jesus first words in His ministry were for people to repent. Sin does exist in the world. If not, why did Jesus have to die because of our sins.

This brings us to the truth, God's Word, the Bible.

In 2 Timothy the Bible says "All scripture is given by inspiration of God, and is profitable for doctrine, for reproof, for correction, and for instruction in righteousness." The Bible is an integral part of our growth and training as Christians. There are many who would like for us to pick and choose which parts of the Bible we should believe and follow. Like the woman Jesus rescued as he shared His message of grace and accountability. God gave us the Bible to follow His one true way to salvation through the death and resurrection of Jesus Christ, and to guide us to a fruitful and abundant life as we grow in our relationship with God.

So as followers of Jesus Christ, we must balance our lives with grace, not condemning; but we must also balance it with truth, God's Word, not watered down or compromised. 2Cor 4:2 says "But we have renounced the hidden things of dishonesty, not walking in craftiness, nor handling the Word of God deceitfully; but by manifestation of the truth commending ourselves to every man's conscience in the sight of God."

Turning 75

Well today is a day you might call a milestone in my life. I turned 75 today. I guess one of the first questions you might ask is how do I feel. I've never been 75 before, so I'm not sure how you are supposed to feel. I know there are some people my age running marathons, while others are going around on motorized scooters. As for me I feel just fine. I have no significant problems physically or mentally (don't go there). To be here today where I live with Kathy and the dogs, and to have the ton of great memories I have. Well I just wouldn't trade that for anything.

I remember when I was a teenager and my grandparents were in their fifties, I thought that was old. Now here I am at 75, not really feeling old at all. I know there are things I can't do physically that I once could, multitasking is difficult, and I have to have my naps from time to time, and my hearing is getting worse, but I really don't feel restricted in any way. Some claim that old people tend to get set in their ways, and kind of rigid when it comes to change. I've got to say that if you have lived on this earth for 75 years, and have been watching, listening and participating in life, and have not formed some strong opinions and principles on key issues in life, you just have not been living at all.

The phrase time does fly comes to mind, and the words are certainly true in my case. One good thing is that most of my memories are good ones. Time seems to have deluded the sad ones that seemed so big at the time. There are so many wonderful memories that spring up out of the blue from time to time that bring a smile to my face and warm my heart.

I believe one of the secrets to how I feel today, is that I've always tried to be and for the most part have been, young at heart. That is something that no date on the calendar or birthday can diminish. I may just get out that "Young At Heart" song by Jimmy Durante to remind me of this.

My faith has been the most important part of my life next to my family. I have shared some of the assurances from the Bible regarding God's provisions earlier in this book. When you talk about true peace, and true joy, and true hope, that is the only place it can be found.

Now I'm thinking about what I have to look forward to in the future. I know there will be some challenges, but there will be some great blessings ahead to. There will be dark days and sunny days. I prefer to look for the brighter picture in all circumstances, and to be a blessing to those I come in contact with for God's glory. I like to think that when people remember me, they will say he made my heart smile. What's the old saying: yesterday's history, tomorrows a mystery, today is a gift from God. Treat it like one.

Bob O'Rear

Electric Vehicles

The people that control the microphones want us to believe that electric vehicles are the greatest thing since sliced bread. That they are the future. They will be cleaner, cheaper and will save our planet. This is the future. It's a no brainer, trust us. There are so many flags and problems with electric vehicles that they don't want us to really think about that I want to talk about. I will give you some facts and statistics, but mostly just some plain old common sense.

Normally when some new or improved technology comes out people are waiting in line to buy it. I don't happen to be one of them, but we're on fixed income and basically happy with what we have. For a lot of people they just can't wait to get the latest cell phone, x-box or big screen tv. When the new cars, SUVs, or trucks come out with all the new and improved technology they want that to, but today vehicles aren't selling like they were. The government is making sure the playing field is not equally balanced, by offering incentives to buy electric vehicles, and making gas and oil more expensive. Some people are freely choosing to go this way, but the vast majority are being forced against our will to buy a product we don't want and can't afford, and that is wrong.

If you want to buy some of the latest technology available, that's fine, but the vehicles we drive are a very different matter. They are an essential part of our economy and survival. Most of us have to have vehicles to get to work and back, to get to the store or doctor's office. When our economy is at it's best, people are on the road. Going to work or school, going shopping, or delivering goods and services. We have planes, trains, and buses moving people from place to place. Things were going pretty well in that area until recently. Then we had executive orders stopping pipelines, and reducing our homeland energy production. We had new bills passes that offered incentives for electric vehicles, and finding new gas and oil at home almost impossible because of the permit process. This was not something the public wanted or demanded. This was something forced down our throats.

The United States has the largest combined gas, oil and coal depositsin the world. We possess the knowledge to build the safest pipelines and build the cleanest energy development. Remember all the changes we've already made to our vehicles, to improve their miles per gallon, and emissions. We must also acknowledge as population and area goes we are a very small part of the world, and they have not signed off on this, so what if any change to the environment is this ultimately going to make. If it was cheaper, safer, better these countries would be at the front of the line. Of course, China and other unfriendly countries will be more than happy to sell us the materials needed to build our $10,000 batteries.

The current cost of these vehicles is more the average person can afford, about twice the cost of an internal combustion engine would cost. Then you come into the problem of resale of an electric vehicle. The average age of an American car is 12 years. At that point the electric vehicle would be on it's third $10,000 battery. Getting someone to take this baby off your hands could prove to be very challenging.

I've saved what I think is by far the biggest problem and greatest drawback to trying to force our country into this new age of electric vehicles: recharging the batteries. I'm afraid that way too many people are of the mind that it will mainly just be a matter of plugging this baby in a recharging station in your home overnight, and then you're good to go the next day. A home charging system requires a 75-amp service.

The average house is equipped with a 100-amp service. On the average residential street the electric infrastructure would be unable to carry more ihan three houses with a single electric vehicle. For half the homes on your block to have electric vehicles, the system would be vastly overloaded. The United Kingdom is already planning for power shortages caused by the charging of electric vehicles. They will calculate when the peak demand will be, determine they will not be able to supply the need, and pre-set the system to not provide power to electric vehicles. Remember in the summer when the temperatures have soared, and the demand for power for air conditioning has caused to grid to almost reach it's peak. Multiply this by a 1000, and tell me where all this extra power is going to magically come from.

Another big problem will be if you decide to go to a power station outside your home. This may prove to be the biggest nightmare of them all. Normally cars time at a gas station is about five minutes. The average time needed to recharge at an electric station is 30 minutes to an hour. This would require six times the surface area that is currently needed by vehicles. Where is this space coming from, and when are you going to recharge. Before work, during your lunch hour, after work. When everybody else is recharging. I am also giving the benefit of the doubt that this station is convenient, and there will not be a line around the block waiting. I bet there isn't one person in a thousand that has the patience to deal with all the waiting and other problems this is going to generate.

I haven't even mentioned long trips for vacations or to visit family or friends, and the problems that would incur. Big government is treating us like little children, telling us they know what is best and forcing this down our throats. Time to wake up America, before it's too late.

Eating Out

This may seem like a lame subject, after you have been reading all the deep insight and fantastic humor that is being shared in other sections of this book, but I think it's important. I mean all across America today, people are asking the same question of their family and friends. Where do you want to go eat?

I remember years ago when our boys were teenagers we would ask them the very same question. Where do you want to go eat? We rarely received any response, so realizing the matter was in my hands, I would suggest a restaurant I thought everyone would enjoy, and someone would inevitably reply that they didn't want to go there. Then I would suggest another place and get the same response. This would cause me to become more and more agitated and frustrated. If I'd been smart I would have said okay we'll just eat at home. Everyone can make their own pb&j or bologna sandwiches. The point of course had been to give their mother a well deserved break, but sometimes the best of plans and intentions don't always work out. I would usually just decide okay we are going to eat at so and so's, and for the most part it worked out okay.

It was on a recent Sunday in our churches parking lot while we were standing around talking to some of our new church family that a great idea occurred to me. By the way, have you ever noticed how at country churches people like to stand around and talk after church. It really is very pleasant and enjoyable. At our old church everyone was rushing to their cars to beat the Baptist to their favorite restaurant. You had to be careful not to get run over in the parking lot. Well the idea occurred to me after hearing some of the conversations in the parking lot where the same question was being asked. Where do you want to go eat? Well the reply was either I don't know, or it don't matter.

I decided it would be a great idea to open up a restaurant and call it I don't Know or It Don't Matter. Then I remembered my 40 years experience in the restaurant industry, and asked myself. Are you crazy? But you are more than welcome to use the idea if you are.

We Were Robbed

No, I'm serious. We were really robbed. Some low down, good for nothing sidewinder snuck into our garage through a side door, while we were home and stole our leaf blower, battery and charger. They also took some decorative pillows from the front porch. Some of you that are not from the south may not be familiar with the word snuck. It's a word derived from words like sneaky, snake, skunk and some other adjectives I want use out of respect for the ladies reading this.

The door they came in through is almost always locked, and was only open because I was working on a project that required me coming in and out of it with a step ladder several times. It wouldn't have taken me so many trips if I had put the battery back in the smoke detector the right way the first time, but I digress. For those of you that might have suffered similar robberies, You certainly have my sympathy. Of course, the bigger issue beyond replacing stolen items, is the invasion of our space and home. We have lived up here for almost five years, and one of the great things about it is the true sense of peace and freedom we have up here. It is so relaxing just sitting on our front porch each day. I will not let some unprincipled moron take that away from us.

As far as I know there have never been any robberies in our subdivision until this happened. All our neighbors have been alerted, and since most of us are at home all day; and we have a first class police force here I expect these brain surgeons to be caught very soon. I doubt that a whack upside the head with my walking stick would help this idiot, but it might make me feel better. I'm really not wired to hurt people that way unless my wife or dogs were threatened, but I will sleep better when they ketch those yahoos.

We have taken extra security, of course, to make sure this doesn't happen again. I really can't afford a new leaf blower every week. I have secured some of my valuable and irreplaceable items in an extremely secure area. I am confident now that even the most cunning of thieves could never find where I have hidden my pet rock and my collection of Slim Whitman albums. There will almost certainly be some security cameras placed at strategic locations in our future.

The items taken was quickly replaced. Most of all, though, I will be eternally grateful, that neither me, my wife nor our pets were injured in any way in this incident. Thank you, Lord.

Bob O'Rear

Adventures

I haven't spent my whole life sitting on the porch. Today I was remembering some of my more adventurous exploits. These are pursuits that are life threatening, but not done recklessly. They are done with people that have the proper training, equipment and expertise. The pursuit itself can then be done with a minimum of risk and a high degre of excitement. The adrenaline rush will make it something to remember, and we can then say look what I just did.

I have been white water rafting 8 times. Half of those times on the Ocoee River where they held the white water Olympic events. The Ocoee was by far the most challenging, and two of those times I was able to share it with my sons. From the look on their faces, I believe they were truly thrilled and excited to have this experience together. This is not something I would consider attempting without an experienced guide to steer and coach us. We were also able to share an overnight rafting trip down the Snake River in Wyoming together. This was not as challenging and dangerous as the Ocoee, but the trip was beautiful and very memorial.

I think the adventure I personally enjoyed the most was the two times I went repelling down the side of a mountain with my oldest son, Casey. I am not at all comfortable with heights. So I just lean back and look up at first. Then take a few steps down to get comfortable. After that it's a blast. A real natural high. Again, I would never attempt something like this without people that have the necessary equipment and expertise to coach me along.

When I was in the army, I joined a sport parachute club at Ft. Bragg and jumped out of a plane at 3,000 feet. This may seem like the most dangerous pursuit, but I didn't consider it that way. First I had a static line connected to my chute that made it open; and if this chute had a problem, I also had a reserve with an altimeter that was set to open at 1,000 feet unless I turned it off. The actual decent just involved enjoying the view. It simply felt like I was hanging from a tree limb as I descended. There was not a real sense of falling at all. After this it was just a matter of landing in an extremely large drop zone. I don't want to _over simplify this, because a girl jumping with us that day broke both her ankles, but at least I can check this off my bucket list.

One other very enjoyable exploit for me was when I was on vacation with Kathy in Destin, Fl. And went parasailing. This is where you are hooked up to a parachute and pulled behind a boat. I was up pretty high, and got a really good view of the whole area. I was up there for over 30 minutes, which gave me plenty of time to enjoy the view and experience. The only scary part was when I was coming in for a landing on the beach. I was coming in way too fast at an angle, and I had no control of the chute. I was convinced I was going to break my leg, but at the last second my decent slowed down, and I landed without any problem on both feet.

Well at 75 those days are behind me, and today my adventures consist of when Kathy talks me into hiking two miles up a mountain to see a waterfall, or riding in my gator with Mattie. I do, however, have these memories of past adventures when I stepped outside my comfort zone.

The Job

As I begin to wrap up the pages of this book, it becomes quite evident to me that in many ways this is somewhat of a biography of my life. If that is indeed true, it occurs to me that I must include one more section that was a very key part of my life. The job I worked at. For forty years, until I retired in 2013, I worked as CFO for a Waffle House franchise.

At our peak we had 50 restaurants, and mine was a newly created job, so basically I created our whole accounting system from the ground up. I was blessed to have two bosses, Gilbert and Dick, that said here is the job, and they just left me alone to get it done. I was also blessed to have three ladies that I hired over a period of time that were the best staff anyone could ever hope to find, Dottie, Michelle and
Jeanette.

I realized early on that the hard working people in the restaurants were the ones who made my job possible, and I always tried to appreciate and look out for them. The daily, weekly and monthly routine of my job were just a part of getting the job done, but the really stimulating and enjoyable times were when I was creating new programs and upgrading systems in our office and in the restaurants.

The two people I worked with in developing these systems, Billy and his wife Kerrie became good friends and a key part of my success. I would conceive of how the reports would look and how they would interface with the other parts of the system, and Billy and Kerrie would write and develop the programs. Sometimes they changes were needed to comply with new laws and sometimes the changes were part of upgrades Waffle House Corporation had made to their system. One of the biggest upgrades we made was when I developed a computer system for our restaurants. The whole system of developing, testing, installing and training was very time consuming and demanding, but in the end extremely rewarding.

During this period of time I was basically working two jobs, but I would always enjoy and be fulfilled during these creative periods.

Dick passed away tragically early in my employment, so Gilbert was my boss during most of my time there. I will be eternally grateful to him for his kindness and generosity during my 40 years at Hillcrest Foods. I believe I was a productive and dependable employee during those years, but I could not have done my job to the extent I did if Gilbert had not given me the resources and trust to do so. This job enabled me to provide for and meet the needs of my family, and use my God given talents in a productive and fulfilling way.

Letter From Home

Dear Son,

I'm writing this slow cause I know you can't read real fast. We don't live where we did when you left. Your dad read in the paper that most accidents happen within twenty miles of home, so we moved. I won't be able to send you the address as the last family that lived here took the numbers with them for their new house, so they wouldn't have to change their address.

This place has a washing machine. The first day I put four shirts in it, pulled the chain; and haven't see 'em since. It only rained twice this week. Three days the first time and four the second.

The coat you wanted me to send you, your aunt Sue said it would be a little too heavy to send in the mail with them heavy buttons, so we cut them off and put them in the pockets.

We got a bill from the funeral home. Said if we didn't make the last payment on grandma's funeral, up she comes.

About your father, He has a lovely new job. He has 500 men under him. He is cutting grass at the cemetery.

About your sister, she had a baby this morning. I haven't found out whether it is a boy or a girl, so I don't know if you are an aunt or an uncle.

Your uncle John fell in the whiskey vat. Some men tried to pull him out, but he fought them off playfully, so he drowned. They cremated him, and he burned for three days.

Three of your friends went off the bridge in a pickup truck. One was driving and the other two were in the back. The driver got out, he rolled down the window and swam to safety. The other two drowned, they couldn't get the tailgate down.

Not much more news this time. Nothing much has happened. Write more later.

Love, Mom

P.S. Was going to send you some money, but the envelope was already sealed.

Precious Memories

It's interesting to me how I remember my life of 75 years. It is mostly filled with pleasant and positive memories. The somewhat painful and unpleasant memories seem to have faded into obscurity. Not completely gone from my memory, but no longer being a front page story, as it seemed to be at the time. I still have regrets for things I said and did, and wish I hadn't given up on some of my more worthy pursuits, but in reality I've had a very good life. I think it's important to dwell on those good memories to truly appreciate how God has richly blessed my life. This will be a shotgun approach as I recall a plethora of things that I remember that still warm my heart and bring a smile to my face.

Holding and rocking our newborn babies. Realizing we had taken on a tremendous responsibility, but embracing the miracle of a new life.

Sitting on my front porch with my dog Mattie and my cup of coffee. Watching the sunrise over the North Georgia Mountains. Fall is just around the corner, and we'll have a front-row seat as the leaves go through their transformation.

The smell in the kitchen and the taste of my grandmothers cooking, always seasoned with love.

When a talented artist and the words of a beautiful hymn come together to reach my soul, and the connection to God becomes very real and incredible. A true blessing from God.

Some visual memories of places we have visited and things we have experienced. The sunset over Montego Bay in an outdoor restaurant with our good friends Harry and Melanie. The view of the Grand Tetons and the lake in front of it from horseback. Riding in a boat at sunset and enjoying the dolphins swimming in unison with us on our last family vacation together in Destin, Fl. So many other times we were blessed to travel to different places and enjoy the works and beauty of God's artistry.

Attending my 50th high school reunion, and realizing what an incredible group of friends and classmates I was privileged to know and grow up with. We were truly the "Greatest Class Alive."

Some of the great places I have eaten at and the great meals I have enjoyed. Fresh seafood at Captain Dave's in Destin. Anytime I have a filet at Longhorns. I've already mentioned the great meals at Mama's table. Fat Matt's BBQ in Atlanta. A Restaurant in Charlotte that is now closed and whose name I can't remember, but their shrimp cocktail sauce and filets were awesome. So many I have left out, but great memories.

Anytime our whole family gets together and everyone is happy and smiling, and things are going well in their life, brings me great pleasure.

My View from the Porch

Adventures with my sons growing up going white water rafting, repelling, camping, jet skiing, and our trips to Wyoming; along with some great family vacations among other memories.

So many fond memories growing up as a boy. Riding my bike all over Red Bank, playing tackle football every Sunday afternoon, hanging out with my friends. Graduating from high school and college. Being raised in, a Christian home, by people who loved me and sat great examples for me.

My 43 year marriage and life with Kathy. We have had a great life together, and have many fond memories. God has truly blessed us, and we look forward to our future years together. There was a time when I was not sure if I would ever have a wife and family, but God had a plan that was sure worth the wait.

We have truly enjoyed spending time with our grandkids, and watching them grow. Don't know how much longer we can keep up with them. We are very pleased to see the young people they are growing up to be. Their parents are doing a great job.

Now I'll just, like the song says mention a few of my favorite things that I might have left out. A laughing baby, the smell of fresh cut grass, the companionship of a good dog, a great song performed by a great entertainer, my team in the championship game, a good sermon, a really good and faithful friend, being appreciated and loved.

This is just a small sample, but hopefully you get the idea." Precious memories, how they linger, how they ever flood my soul."

My Creed

This is a creed I have kind of adopted. I would also suggest Longfellow's "A Psalm of Life. Whether or not I've lived up to this creed in any way is not for me to say. Anyway I consider it a worthwhile goal.

My Creed

"I would be true, for there are those who trust me;
I would be pure, for there are those who care;
I would be strong, for there is much to suffer,
I would be brave, for there is much to dare.

I would be friend to all-the foe, the friendless;
I would be giving and forget the gift.
I would be humble, for I know my weakness;
I would look up-and laugh-and-love-and lift."

Howard Walter Arnold